Captain Funny Pants
Presents

CLEVER JOKES FOR CLEVER KIDS

By Aaron T. Arthur

All of the characters and representations in this book are fictitious, and any resemblance to actual persons, living or dead, is purely coincidental.

PUBLICATION HISTORY

First publication date December 2018

CAPTAIN FUNNY PANTS PRESENTS
CLEVER JOKES FOR CLEVER KIDS

All rights reserved.

Copyright © 2018 by Punchline Press

Cover design and Captain Funny Pants character © 2018 by Punchline Press

Treasure Map Deadhand font by GemFonts and Phoenix Phonts

Pirate Scroll and Ship vectors by vecteezy.com

No part of this book may be reproduced or transmitted in any form or by any means, electronic or mechanical, including photocopying, or by any information storage or retrieval system, without written permission from the publisher.

For information address:

info@punchlinepress.com

For general information visit:

punchlinepress.com

ISBN: 978-0-9937106-7-4

Thank you for buying this book!

Be sure to join the mailing list to receive info on new releases and other awesome updates.

Ask your parents to sign up at punchlinepress.com

If you really like this book, be sure to leave a review on the retailer's website where you bought it. I'd really appreciate it!

Contents

Question & Answer 1

One-Liners 42

Long Form Jokes 64

What's in a Name? 71

Knock Knock Jokes 77

Makes You Think 86

Question & Answer

Q: Why are three people with glasses so cold?
A: They're eyes cubed.

Q: What do you call two banana peels on the floor?
A: A pair of slippers.

Q: When was dinner served?
A: Before it was ate.

Q: Why was the chef so interested in the barbecue competition?
A: He had a steak in it.

Q: How do turtles start a race?
A: Ready, Set, Slow!

Q: How do nuts sneeze?
A: ca-SHEW!

Q: What's the difference between a car ride and a canoe ride?
A: The canoe ride is a rowed trip.

Q: What's the worst snack for your windshield?
A: Chips!

Q: What did the pickle say at the poker tournament?
A: Dill me in.

Q: What do well-trained dogs and Shakespearean quandaries have in common?
A: They give us pause.

Q: Why did the director tell his actors to break a leg?
A: He wanted to sign an all new cast.

Q: Why was the door scared?
A: It was alarmed.

Q: How do you watch a car crash?
A: Through a collide-o-scope!

Q: What do you get if you run over a genie?
A: Three squishes!

Q: What goes in goblin glasses?
A: Gremlenses.

Q: What do you call a steak that's just returned from finishing school?
A: Well seasoned.

Q: What do champions clean their teeth with?
A: Olympicks!

Q: Why did Hemingway keep so many cats?
A: Because he needed the mews.

Q: What's the difference between Elvis and Jay-Z?
A: Elvis was a hip-pop star!

Q: What is the loudest color?
A: YELLow!

Q: What was the psychologist's advice to the claustrophobic pickle?
A: Just dill with it.

Q: How do you pass bulldozer school?
A: Get a good grade!

Q: How do you start a letter to a rodent?
A: Deer mouse.

Q: What did the teddy bear say when offered dessert?
A: No thanks. I'm stuffed.

Clever Jokes for Clever Kids

Q: How do you stop a rhino from charging?
A: Take away its credit card.

Q: How did the tomato get to the show?
A: She took a taxi cabbage.

Q: How do chickens write a melody?
A: On a cluckenspiel.

Q: Have you seen the new movie about crows?
A: Critics are raven.

Q: What did the spicy beef burrito say to the matador with IBS?
A: "The hunter has become the hunted!"

Q: Did you hear about the new Batman movie?
A: It got pretty bat ratings.

Q: How do you make submarine bread?
A: Torpedough.

Q: How do German bakers start complaining?
A: "You know what's the wurst?"

Q: Who does the Giblet King call?
A: His livery servants.

Q: What do you call a picture of a Roman?
A: A pho-toga-raph.

Q: Did you hear about the chemistry class for weightlifters?
A: The periodic table only has iron on it.

Q: Where did the baby birds work?
A: At the chick-out counter.

Q: What type of boatmen are you most likely to find in the ceiling?
A: Rafters!

Q: How can you tell if you ran over a mouse?
A: The wheel squeaks.

Q: Where does corn buy pants?
A: The husky section.

Q: What's Captain Kirk's favorite hockey play?
A: A slap shot!

Q: Why did the cross-eyed teacher get fired?
A: He couldn't contol his pupils.

Q: Where do lions keep their socks?
A: DROARS!

Q: What's the hardest part of digging clams?
A: The wading is the hardest part.

Q: Where do nuts go to the bathroom?
A: The pecan.

Q: What do trees do before they smooch?
A: They put on lip sticks.

Q: What do you call a cow with two legs?
A: Lean beef.

Q: What do you call a cow with no legs?
A: Ground beef.

Q: What do you call a cow lying in a hole?
A: Udder ground.

Q: Where did the cold firefighter come down from?
A: The North Pole!

Q: What's the best flavor of pickled flowers?
A: Daffodill.

Q: Which cat's spots are always falling off?
A: Leperd.

Q: What do you put on a wounded chicken?
A: A poultrice.

Q: Why did the salesman wear a raincoat?
A: It was slicker.

Q: Who is the best smelling cowboy hero?
A: The Cologne Ranger.

Q: How do you get into a gorilla cage?
A: Monkeys!

Q: Who peels the veggies at the zoo?
A: The pare-it!

Q: Did you hear about the coffee in the alley?
A: It got mugged.

Q: What board game do aggressive hockey coaches prefer?
A: Checkers.

Clever Jokes for Clever Kids

Q: What do you call knocked out bread?
A: Coma-toast!

COMA TOAST

Q: What's the smelliest part of the sun?
A: The solar wind!

Q: What does the sun keep in its trunk for emergencies?
A: Solar flares.

Q: What do small beards taste like?
A: A little goaty.

Q: What do you call a nervous monkey?
A: Chimp-antsy!

Q: What do bakers keep in the car for emergencies?
A: Pie-lons!

Q: Where do lions live?
A: Maine.

Q: What do punctuation and yoga have in common?
A: Calm ahh's.

Q: What do birds need to go skydiving?
A: A parrot-chute!

Q: Why did the dirigible pilot hide in the bathroom?
A: He had a blimple.

Q: What's the most popular instrument for philosophers?
A: The why-o-lin.

Q: How do commandos make salad?
A: They get to the chopper.

Q: What does the lottery and a wall have in common?
A: Win dough.

Q: What do horn players wear on their feet?
A: Tuba socks!

Q: Why did the chicken cross the road?
A: It was a priest chicken blessing the driveway to his new church.

Q: What do messengers wear to bed?
A: Page-amas.

Q: What did the zoo keeper wear to the business meeting?
A: Suit and tiger!

Q: How do ships enter the dockyard?
A: They barge in!

Q: Which fruit can fly a spaceship?
A: A coconaut!

Q: How do modern fisherman catch fish?
A: They use the net.

Q: How do annelids contribute to climate change?
A: Global worming!

Q: What part of the mushroom makes rodents extra squeaky?
A: The mice-helium!

Q: What do Jewish holy men do when they're tired?
A: Rub eyes!

Q: What's the difference between a bodybuilder and a bandit?
A: Bodybuilders are high-whey men.

Q: Why did Athena go to the mechanic?
A: Scheduled owl change.

Q: Why was the detective not interested in the tiny pickle found at the crime scene?
A: It was no big dill.

Q: Where did the tiny frog check his email?
A: On his li'l i-pad.

LI'L i-PAD

Q: What's the difference between Hamlet and Nikola Tesla?
A: Tesla was going off about more tall coils.

Q: What's the hardest question to ponder at the water slides?
A: Tubey or not tubey?

Q: Which actress can do whatever she wants?
A: Carte Blanchette!

Q: What do acrobats eat for breakfast?
A: Tra-pease porridge!

Q: What happened to the Scottish snitch?
A: Got kilt.

Q: What's the difference between parking beside a Rolls-Royce and parking under a UFO?
A: If you park under the UFO you might get Grey poop on.

Q: How's the parmesan?
A: Grate!

Q: What bird don't you mess with?
A: Steven Seagull!

Q: Why did the pharaohs keep building bigger buildings?
A: Pyramid pressure!

Q: How do you make a noodle chain?
A: With link-guine!

Q: What's the saddest dinosaur?
A: Tear Rex.

Q: Did you hear about the depressed harpooner?
A: He was so sad he was whaling.

Q: What's the opposite of a minion?
A: A minyang.

Q: What did the minty clock say?
A: Tic-Tac.

Q: Did you hear about the mathematician who was afraid of negative numbers?
A: He stops at nothing to avoid them.

Q: What did the moon send to the sea at Christmas?
A: You'll tide greetings!

Q: How does a squirrel get a good sleep?
A: It finds a comfy willow!

Q: Where do eagles look when they don't know a word?
A: Diction aerie!

Q: How do you marry a restaurant hostess?
A: You ring the door belle.

Q: What do fabulous astronauts do with a great outfit?
A: Rocket!

Q: What do tree surgeons hang on their windows?
A: Pruning sheers!

Q: Where does salad change into something more comfortable?
A: Behind the dressing screen!

Q: What's the freshest dinosaur?
A: Minty Rex!

Q: What do you call a pirate in a bottle?
A: Capped in.

Q: Why do opinionated cows stick together?
A: They want to be herd.

Q: Did you hear about Charles Dickens' lesser known book about estimating travel time with the London cab system?
A: It's called "Wait Expectations."

Q: What school subject sends Millennials to safe spaces more often than any other subject?
A: Triggernometry.

Q: What did the composer add to his laptop to make it faster?
A: Eight gigues of Brahms.

Q: What has four wheels and flies?
A: A garbage truck.

Q: Did you hear about the pee Olympics?
A: Because urinal the events!

Q: Did you hear the one about the blind lettuce farmer?
A: He found it hard to get a head.

Clever Jokes for Clever Kids

Q: Where do you find funny recipes?
A: In a kook-book!

Q: Why is the tomato red?
A: Because it saw the salad dressing.

Q: What fruit can you find at the end of a rope?
A: A pull!

Q: How do you hide a dromedary?
A: Camel-flage.

Q: How do you turn a bull around?
A: Steer the other way.

Q: What do you call a soft metal flying dinosaur?
A: Pteroductile!

Q: Do you know why horse-food stores are so bad at taking criticism?
A: They hate getting any kind of feed back.

Q: What kind of jokes do legs like?
A: Fun, knee ones.

Q: What did the ruler say to his physician?
A: Give it to me straight, doc.

Q: What do you call a can on a pirate's head?
A: Cap-tin.

Q: What do hot chickens drink?
A: Nest-tea.

Q: How do you know the ingredients in a sleeping cow?
A: Read the lay bull.

Q: What did Little Miss Muffet bring to baby Jesus?
A: A whey in the manger.

Q: What's the best time of year to buy a mattress?
A: Spring.

Q: What do aspirins sleep on?
A: Pill-ows!

Q: Why did the giraffes get kicked out of prom?
A: For necking!

Q: What do sporty roosters drive?
A: Chicken coupes!

Q: Why don't cannibals eat clowns?
A: They taste funny!

Q: What do you call an old English leg?
A: Thy.

Q: What do geriatric 1990's cavemen drive?
A: Buick LeSabretooth.

Q: What did the rhinoceros get at the post office?
A: Stamps.

Q: What did the knight get from the postman?
A: Nothing but chainmail.

Q: What color is the wind?
A: Blue.

Q: How do mules open doors?
A: With a donkey.

Q: Why did the sailor eat the canapé?
A: Captain's hors d'oeuvres.

Q: How do comedians get off the floor?
A: They standup.

Q: Why are cooks mean?
A: Because they beat the eggs and whip the cream!

Q: What kind of shoes do bakers wear?
A: Loafers!

Q: How did the kosher deli beat the competition?
A: With a ruthless schmear campaign.

Q: What do you call a holy squirrel?
A: A chipmonk!

Q: When does corn stay up until midnight?
A: New Ears Eve.

Q: What did Aristotle amuse himself with as a child?
A: Play-toh.

Q: How do you buy a dark web page?
A: Go through a real-TOR.

Q: Why couldn't the pirate charge his cell phone?
A: He couldn't find "A/Sea" adapter.

Q: How do pirates text?
A: i-patch-Phone.

Q: What happens when a pirate reaches light speed?
A: Yarr, he achieves critical mast!

Q: Skunk philosophy?
A: Exi-stench-alism.

Q: How do knights swear?
A: They use the s-word.

Q: What do resistors have for lunch?
A: Ohmlettes.

Q: What did the oak dip his chicken wing in?
A: Branch dressing.

Q: Did you hear about the Italian chef?
A: He pasta way.

Q: Why did the candy manufacturer hire a psychiatrist?
A: They needed to make their product in a nut-free facility.

Clever Jokes for Clever Kids

Q: What do you call a confused lumberjack?
A: Stumped!

Q: What do you call bees with ears?
A: Bears!

Q: What do you say to a slow hot dog?
A: Ketchup!

Q: Why did the treasure map lead to the former Mrs. Blackbeard's house?
A: Because the ex marks the spot.

Q: Why did the pirate have to change his window?
A: Because there was a big Kraken it.

Q: What did the ocean say to the sky?
A: Nothing. It just waved.

Q: Why is Fozzie Bear such a good gambler?
A: He knows when to hold 'em and when to wakka wakka wakkaway.

Q: Why did the yogurt go to cheese school?
A: He was there on a cultural exchange program.

One - Liners

I stopped at the bank today.
I stopped myself from robbing the bank.

It's hard to be a dog.
They look like they have a ruff life.

Noah's story had quite the arc.

Don't talk back to bakers.
It's too easy to get a rise out of them.

The hole digger's business was doing well.

I saw a sheep fall off a cliff.
Better ewe than me.

Don't worry about the fog coming in.
It mist last time.

Usually, the Quidditch match is won
by the team that wands it more.

I can't sail, canoe?

People sure love French-Canadian maple
syrup, but I think it's d'erable.

Remote controls are such snobs.
So clicky.

Grapes don't usually complain, but if you
step on them they might wine a little.

If you try to canoe around a castle, your boat might need a moat oar.

Saw a barber on a horse.
Clip-clop.

Archaeological jokes are getting really old.

The first day of bagpipe school you're told
not to run with the bagpipes.
You could put an aye out, or worse, get kilt.

The news of a killer fish on the loose
came as a shark to everyone.

Pork salesmen travel bacon forth.

Daily war trivia is random facts of violence.

When playing shoe poker,
the best hand is all laces.

There have been tough times in
the school's Astronomy Club,
but things are looking up now.

I like to tell Dad jokes and sometimes
he laughs.

Arabian Kings love sultan pepper wings.

Don't worry if you lose your veggies.
They'll turnip eventually.

Constipated Olympians race for the Prodiem.

Shaking hands with pirates is amazing.
Try it once and you'll be hooked.

Saw a thief on horseback.
Clops and robbers.

I went to a butter knife show.
It was quite dull.

I saw a dog with no back legs.
It had a little wheelchair.
It made me sad, but his tail was a wagon.

Chemists addicted to coffee don't see
coffee as a problem.
It's a solution.

The gangsters heard the cops outside
their secret moonshine cellar.
They held still.

The student couldn't remember
what Pavlov was famous for,
but the name rang a bell.

The cabinet maker's union strike
is unfortunate.
They woodwork if they could.

Overheard at the caveman restaurant: "If you've never eaten dinosaur before, you should triceratops."

Technology before the abacus was unreliable. You couldn't count on anything.

After moderate success in his first year as a sole proprietor, Blackbeard decided to incor-pirate.

Quality dinnerware, once hard to acquire, is now common-plates.

How do pirates settle workplace disputes?
They involve H – Arrrrrrr!

The beekeeper was so stressed
he had hives.

Intriguing fugitives in hats are
capped-evading.

Be careful buying German pastries,
they might be Stollen.

A good hotdog is something to relish.

I wasn't eating corn that long,
but it felt like a whole ear.

Two wrongs don't make a right,
but three lefts do.

Anyone out there named Phil?
Ever considered naming your kid Refill?

I saw a car in the bathroom.
It was stalled.

Jokes about ore are a gold mine!

Aaron T. Arthur

I saw a horse in outer space.
It had a saddle light.

A church bell fell on a baby goat
and it barely made a sound.
Just kid-ding.

Smart people like elevator jokes.
They work on lots of levels.

If the melons want the dowry
they cantaloupe.

I split my dessert with my ex.
It was shared custardy.

A typo walks into a bra.

Aaron T. Arthur

My father said his attention could only be held by one sport in particular.
He said it was in-golfing.

A giggling blizzard is
snow laughing matter.

Egg farmers with low productivity are facing a crack-down.

Police made a grizzly discovery.
It was a bear.

After the fall of feudalism,
all the fonts were sans-serf.

The interview with the entomologist revealed how sloppy the journalist was. There were lots of misquote-os.

I was at a picnic with my parents. There was also an ant on my mom's side.

Szechuan rooster is cock of the wok.

Is anecdotal evidence reliable? One man says "yes."

The cat's social blunder was a true faux paw.

Font design really took off after Microsoft introduced Arial.

Never trust an atom.
They make up everything.

Explaining puns to kleptomaniacs is hard because they always take things literally.

Disorganized librarians can benefit from shelf help books.

Non-Euclidean geometry is hard to figure out.

Snares are nifty can-trap-shins.

Math students shouldn't use a calculator at the first sine of trouble.

I've always wanted to build a snowman on an iceberg ever since I heard that snowman is an island.

Marathon humor is a long-running joke.

You've got to hand it to short people sometimes because they can't reach the top shelf.

Attendance at the witch doctor's "Voodoo Resurrection" course is on the rise.

Be careful not to dump cayenne or chili
powder into a river, lake or waterway,
because they are invasive spices.

What's the secret to telling jokes timing.

Learning Braille isn't impossible,
but there are a few bumps along the way.

If you find it difficult to explain something
during a conversation, you might need to
get out a pen and paper to get it write.

The mess hall in the French prison was
serving chicken cordoned off.

There once was a German child
who was kind.
All his friends were Kinder.

People with a phobia of escalators
will take steps to avoid them.

If you ever decide to bleach your hair
blond, don't be surprised if you feel
light-headed.

Magnetic jewelry makes you
more attractive.

The smartest dinosaur is thesaurus.

There are so many options
at the wine store.
I've narrowed it down to rosé and rose B.

ROSÉ OR ROSE B?

Long Form Jokes

The student said that his teacher drank too much coffee, adding, "why do you even drink it? Coffee is just a bitter bean." To which the teacher angrily replied, "that's grounds for suspension!"

I told my doctor I couldn't poop, so she handed me a pair of cut-off shorts.
I said: "what's this?"
She said: "ex-slacks."

A bull turned to his friend and said, "I'm really worried about getting Mad Cow disease."
"I'm not worried about that at all," the friend said.
The bull was puzzled. "Why is that?" he asked.
The friend replied, "because I'm a tractor."

A frantic patient told his doctor, "You have to help me! I'm a wigwam! I'm a teepee! I'm a wigwam! I'M A TEEPEE!"
The doctor calmed the patient down. "It's okay," the doctor said. "I know what's wrong with you. You're just two tents."

"The Captain's Pants"

Captain Blackbeard and his crew were sailing the seven seas. The barrelman called down from the crow's nest. "Ahoy! Enemy ship straight ahead!"

Blackbeard turned to his first mate and said, "yarr, fetch me my red coat."

"Why your red coat, Captain?"

"If the enemy injures me, the crew won't see my blood, and they will keep fighting," Blackbeard replied. "Now quit wasting time and fetch me my red coat!"

The crew valiantly fought off the enemy and escaped with their lives.

The next day the barrelman called down from the crow's nest. "Ahoy! Two enemy ships straight ahead!"

Blackbeard turned to his first mate and said, "yarr, fetch me my red coat."

Without hesitation, the first mate went to fetch the captain's red coat.

Again, the crew valiantly fought off the enemy and escaped with their lives.

The next day the barrelman called down from the crow's nest. "Ahoy! TEN enemy ships straight ahead!"

Blackbeard turned to his first mate and said, "yarr, fetch me my brown pants."

"Peg Leg, Hook, and Patch"

A young buccaneer wandered into the pirate hangout one day. He sat down at a table next to an old pirate with a peg for a leg, a hook for a hand, and a patch over one eye. Curious, he turned to the pirate and asked, "would you mind telling me how you got the peg-leg?"

The pirate, always willing to share a tale of high-seas adventure, loudly answered, "Yarr! I was sailing the high seas when a rogue wave sent me over the port bow. A hungry shark attacked! I fought him tooth and nail! He took me leg, but I got him in the end and feasted on shark soup that same night!"

"Wow!" replied the buccaneer. He was so impressed he bought the pirate some food and drink. "May I ask how you got the hook for a hand?"

"Yarr!" growled the pirate, proudly. "I was sailing the high seas, when out of the fog comes a mighty warship! They attempted to board us and plunder our treasure! I fiercely fought the ship's captain with me saber. He took me hand, but I got him in the end, and we won the day!"

"Wow! Amazing!" the buccaneer exclaimed, infatuated with the old pirate's tales that kept getting better and better. He bought even more food and drink for the pirate who was reveling in the attention. "What an incredible life you've lived, Mr. Pirate. Finally, may I ask how you got the eye-patch?"

"Yarr," the pirate said, somewhat sadly. "I was sailing the high seas. It was a fine day with not a cloud in the sky. I lifted me face to the warm sunshine when a gull flew overhead and pooped in me eye."

"Oh," the buccaneer said, not expecting such a bad luck story. "I didn't realize seagull poop could make someone lose an eye. That's pretty sad, and I guess I'll be more careful around seagulls now, right?"

The pirate hung his head and replied, "Yarr… 'twas not the seagull poop…"

"No?" the buccaneer replied, eager to hear more harrowing tales.

"No," said the pirate. "Sigh, 'twas the first day with me hook…"

What's in a Name?

Q: What do you call a retired grave digger?
A: Doug.

Q: What do you call a guy with a rubber toe?
A: Roberto.

Q: What do you call a guy on the radio?
A: Roger.

Q: What do you call a lock-picker?
A: Jimmy.

Q: What do you call a guy who used to sketch?
A: Drew.

Q: What do you call a guy who is always on the phone?
A: Colin.

Q: What do you call a guy chasing a fighter jet?
A: SAM!

Q: What do you call an armless, legless water-skier?
A: Chum.

Q: What do you call a guy eating an apple?
A: Cory.

Q: What do you call a guy in a recording studio?
A: Mike.

Q: What do you call a guy who doesn't care?
A: Whatever you want.

Q: What do you call two guys hanging over a window?
A: Kurt and Rod.

Q: What do you call a guy who is stuck in a hole?
A: Phil.

Q: What do you call a woman who is stuck in a hole?
A: Peg.

Q: What do you call a guy sitting in a pile of leaves?
A: Russell.

Q: What do you call a guy in the middle of a lake?
A: Bob.

Q: What do you call a guy who is hanging on a wall?
A: Art.

Q: What do you call a woman who likes to insult people?
A: Barb.

Q: What do you call a guy in a catapult?
A: Chuck.

Q: What do you call a guy strong enough to lift a car?
A: Jack.

Q: What do you call a guy who has just been attacked by a cat?
A: Claude.

Q: What do you call a guy who is simmering in a pot?
A: Stew.

Q: What do you call a mechanical horse?
A: Roboclop.

Q: What do you call a guy with a feather in his forehead?
A: Fletch.

Knock Knock Jokes

Knock, knock.
  Who's there?
Can opener.
  Can opener who?
Unlock the door. I can opener.

Knock, knock.
  Who's there?
Atch.
  "Atch" who?
GESUNDHEIT!

Knock, knock.
   Who's there?
Never!
   Never who?
Never gonna give you up, never gonna let you down, never gonna run around and desert you.

Knock knock.
   Who's there?
Pee.
   Pee who?
Who farted?

Knock knock.
   Who's there?
Lettuce.
   Lettuce who?
Lettuce in! It's cold outside.

Knock knock.
Who's there?
Boo.
Boo who?
Don't cry. It's only me.

Knock knock.
Who's there?
Vacuum cleaner salesman.
Vacuum cleaner salesman who?
Let me in. It sucks outside.

Knock knock.
Who's there?
Interrupting cow.
Interrupt…
MOO!!!

Knock knock.
   Who's there?
Who.
   Who who?
Was that an owl?

Knock knock.
 Who's there?
Jimmy.
 Jimmy who?
Jimmy the door. It's stuck!

Knock knock.
 Who's there?
Been.
 Been who?
Been a while. I'm not surprised you don't remember me.

Knock knock.
 Who's there?
Beats.
 Beats who?
Beats me!

Knock knock.
   Who's there?
Tree.
   Tree who?
Wood you mind if I came inside?

Knock knock.
   Who's there?
Corn.
   Corn who?
Army corn.
   Army corn?
Yes, please open the door. I'm important.
   How important?
I'm a kernel.

Knock knock.
 Who's there?
Police! Open the door!
 Well, only if you ask nicely…
Pretty police?!

Knock knock.
 Who's there?
Sweet potato.
 Oh, are you here for the Thanksgiving party?
Yes, I yam!

Knock knock.
 Who's there?
Mustard.
 Mustard who?
Sorry, I mustard got the wrong address.

Knock knock.
   Who's there?
Mural painter.
   Mural painter who?
Let me in.
It's cold, and I'm going to frieze!

Knock knock.
   Who's there?
Little old lady.
   Little old lady who?
I didn't know you could yodel!

Knock knock.
   Who's there?
Kangar.
   Kangar who?
Boing!

Knock knock.
  Who's there?
Tomatoes, beans, ground beef and spices.
  Tomatoes, beans, ground beef and spices who?
Let us in. It's chili outside!

Knock knock.
  Who's there?
Novel.
  Novel who?
It's a long story.

Knock knock.
  Who's there?
Canoe.
  Canoe who?
Canoe please let me in?

Makes You Think

Q: What gets bigger the more you take away from it?
A: A hole in the ground.

Q: What sucks more the less it sucks?
A: A vacuum.

Q: Why did the elephant paint his toenails?
A: To hide in the bag of M&Ms.
Q: Have you ever seen an elephant in a bag of M&Ms?
See! It works!

Q: Why are elephants big, gray and wrinkly?
A: Because if they were small, white and round, they'd be an Aspirin.

Q: How do pigeons ask for money?
A: "Can you sparrow dollar?"

Aaron T. Arthur

Q: Where do elephants get their lunch?
A: At the cafeteria like everyone else!

Are Spanish dinner theater performers tapa-dancers?

The meaning of opaque is unclear.

Never judge a song by its cover.

We don't know if dogs love trees or just bark.

The weirdest thing about wheat is how it's Spelt.

The baker kept his marriage fresh
by always bringing home flours.

Do bee marines get buzz cuts?

Spice traders are like thyme travelers.

Mind bender:
what is the opposite of a banana peel?

I don't know why people go
shopping on Black Friday.
Everyone knows that best-deal day
is July 14th.

How does AM radio
keep working after noon?

Do spiders that live outside the United
States have 2.44 meters instead of 8 feet?

Is it safe to ground your kids
during a thunderstorm?

If we get a new moon every thirty days,
why does it always look so
old and cratered?

Even without a plastic jacket,
you get a rain coat.

What sound did the apple make
when it hit Newton's head?

THUNK!

From the Author

I would like to thank you again for purchasing this book.

I love a good joke. Who doesn't? I tell jokes to anyone who will listen, so what better way to spread the laughter than to write them down for the whole world to read!

You might find that some people don't appreciate your sense of humor, but that's okay. Jokes are only for people who like to have fun and enjoy life.

This collection is the result of years and years of crafting and gathering jokes. After all that time, here is what I've learned:

The more often you tell jokes,
the funnier your life gets!

It's true!

The best way to write a new joke is to tell the jokes you already know. In fact, I've already started writing my next joke book. Ask your parents to sign up for my mailing list, and I'll let them know when the next book comes out!

In the meantime, if you like this book, be sure to leave a review on the retailer's website where you bought it. I'd really appreciate it! Until next time, keep laughing and keep telling jokes!

Sincerely,

Aaron T. Arthur

www.ingramcontent.com/pod-product-compliance
Lightning Source LLC
Chambersburg PA
CBHW050441010526
44118CB00013B/1624